When I look at you

My book about feelings

by Karen Collum - Illustrated by Lorenzo Sabbatini

Sometimes when I look at you,
Your hands are clenched tight,
Your eyes are crinkled up

And your feet are stamping.
I think you might be feeling angry.

When do you feel angry?

'Do not let the sun go down
while you are still angry.'
Ephesians 4:26

Sometimes when I look at you,
Your hands hang by your sides,

Your eyes are watering
And your mouth is frowning.
I think you might be feeling sad.

When do you feel sad?

'Jesus wept.'
John 11:35

Sometimes when I look at you,
Your eyes are bright,
Your mouth is smiling

And your voice is laughing.
I think you might be feeling happy.

When do you feel happy?

'A cheerful heart is good medicine.'
Proverbs 17:22

Sometimes when I look at you,
Your body is small,

Your eyes are looking at the floor
And your mouth is frowning.
I think you might be feeling lonely.

When do you feel lonely?

'God has said,
Never will I leave you; never will I forsake you.'
Hebrews 13:5

Sometimes when I look at you,
Your eyes are open wide,
Your heart is pounding

And your feet want to run.
I think you might be feeling scared.

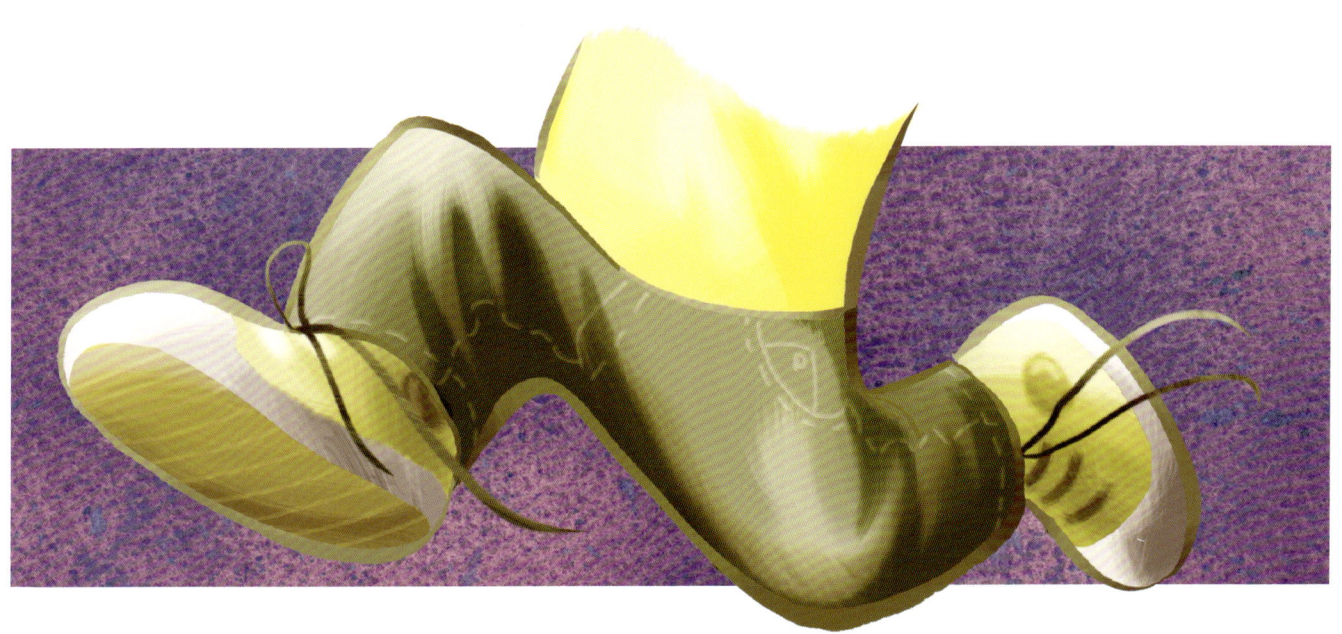

When do you feel scared?

'The LORD is with me:
I will not be afraid.'
Psalms 118:6

Sometimes when I look at you,
Your face is red,
Your eyes are looking the other way

And you try to hide behind your hands.
I think you might be feeling embarrassed.

When do you feel embarrassed?

'Man looks at the outside,
but the LORD looks at the heart.'
1 Samuel 16:7

Sometimes when I look at you,
Your hands are twisted together,
Your tummy is squirming,

Your feet are fidgeting.
I think you might be feeling nervous.

When do you feel nervous?

'Trust in the LORD
with all your heart.'
Proverbs 3:5

Sometimes when I look at you,
Your mouth is smiling,
Your hands are clapping

And your feet won't stay still.
I think you might be feeling excited.

When do you feel excited?

'We are looking forward to a new heaven and a new earth. . . .'
2 Peter 3:13

There are lots of different feelings.

'So God created man in his own image . . .'
Genesis 1:27

How are you feeling right now?

First published in 2011

Copyright © 2011 Autumn House Publishing (Europe) Ltd

All rights reserved. No part of this publication may be reproduced
in any form without prior permission from the publisher.

British Library Cataloguing in Publication Data.
A catalogue record for this book is available from the British Library.

ISBN 978-1-906381-97-4

Published by Autumn House (Europe),
Grantham, Lincolnshire.

Illustrated by Lorenzo Sabbatini.

Printed in Thailand.